Channcey Marvin Cady

Parlor Gems

A choice selection of music, instrumental and vocal, by the best composers, to which is added original charades for parlor performance

Channcey Marvin Cady

Parlor Gems

A choice selection of music, instrumental and vocal, by the best composers, to which is added original charades for parlor performance

ISBN/EAN: 9783337427450

Printed in Europe, USA, Canada, Australia, Japan

Cover: Foto ©Thomas Meinert / pixelio.de

More available books at **www.hansebooks.com**

XIIIth Thousand.

A

Choice Selection of Music,

INSTRUMENTAL AND VOCAL,

BY THE

BEST COMPOSERS,

TO WHICH IS ADDED ORIGINAL

CHARADES FOR PARLOR PERFORMANCE.

BY

C. M. CADY.

NEW YORK:
PUBLISHED BY THE AUTHOR, C. M. CADY,
107 DUANE STREET.
1879.

CHAMPION
(Spouting Spring)
NATURAL WATER
FROM SARATOGA.
FOR SALE BY ALL RESPECTABLE DRUGGISTS AND DEALERS IN MINERAL WATERS.

The CHAMPION SPOUTING SPRING contains a very large preponderance of the elements which render mineral waters valuable as medicine, and which are in constant use by Physicians of the various schools; and the remarkable cure of some of the prevailing diseases has given the water of this Spring great favor among professional men. For *Headache*, or disordered state of the Stomach arising from the use of wine or hearty eating, it is a fine corrective, giving immediate relief. It is invaluable for the treatment of Biliousness, Dyspepsia, Constipation, Piles, Rheumatism, Neuralgia, Cutaneous Diseases, Scrofula, &c., and owing to the presence of Lithia, Magnesia and Bi-Carbonate of Lime, is recommended by Physicians for Bright's Disease of the Kidneys, and Diseases of the Bladder.

DIRECTIONS.—As a cathartic, take half a pint or more, as experience may dictate, before breakfast, and at a moderately high temperature, if prompt action is desired. As a tonic, half a glass three or four times a day, between meals. As the cathartic principles of the CHAMPION WATER are double those of the Congress Spring, only half the quantity is required.

The constant and increasing success of the CHAMPION WATER is due to its hygienic properties; it is *refreshing* and *healthful*, and should be found in every home.

ORDERS ADDRESSED TO

PARK & TILFORD, New York City.
E. J. HART & CO., No. 73—79 Tchoupitoulas Street, N. O., La.
JONES & SIBLEY, Cor. 5th and Market Street, St. Louis, Mo.
J. & E. N. BLOCKI, No. 20 Market Street, Chicago, Ill.
H. C. GAYLORD, No. 110 Monument Square, Cleveland, O.
COLEMAN & ROGERS, No. 168 West Baltimore St., Baltimore, Md.

W. H. BROWN & BRO., No. 25 South Sharp Street, Baltimore, Md.
G. G. CORNELL, Penn Avenue, Washington, D. C.
STOTT & CROMWELL, Penn Avenue, Washington, D. C.
BULLOCK & CRENSHAW, No. 528 Arch Street, Philadelphia, Pa.
FREDERICK BROWN, Cor. 5th and Chestnut St., Philadelphia, Pa.
S. S. PIERCE, Cor. Court and Tremont Street, Boston, Mass.

CARTER, HARRIS & HAWLEY, No. 156 Washington Street, Boston.

TO MY FRIEND,

SAMUEL T. HILLMAN, ESQ., OF NEW YORK,

THIS WORK IS RESPECTFULLY DEDICATED.

PREFACE.

It has been my aim to present in this book the best selection of music extant, for parlor use, and afford it at a price so low as to be within the reach of all. It includes instrumental and vocal morceaux, ranging in difficulty from easy to moderately difficult, and in quality from the popular and brilliant to the standard and classical, but each of its kind a GEM. *In thus seeking a variety of the best music from the best and most popular authors, I have made the discovery that Beethoven, Mozart, Mendelssohn, Schumann, Schubert, Chopin, Strauss, Auber, Offenbach, Gounod, Kucken, Sullivan, Hullah, and the other composers represented in this collection have really written better than I ever did, and therefore the book contains no effusions of my own. No doubt many thousands of musical people will be the happier for it. Let the fact of the above discovery be neatly worked into my epitaph. It is hoped that this grave sentiment may impart to my prologue the solemnity so eagerly sought for in every well regulated preface.*

New York, May 15, 1875.   C. M. C.

TABLE OF CONTENTS.

INSTRUMENTAL.

1. Flying Dutchman............................Arranged by *Himan.*
2. Recollections of a Music Box............................*Pape.*
3. Amaryllis............................Arranged by A. H. *Pease.*
4. Traumerei............................*Schumann.*
5. Anvil Chorus, Il Trovatore............................*Verdi.*
6. The Happy Farmer............................*Schumann.*
7. L'Escarpolette, (swing song)............................*Fontaine.*
8. Ecossaisen. Opus 18, No. 2............................*Schubert.*
9. Beautiful Blue Danube. Waltz............................*Strauss.*
10. Petite Tarantelle............................*Heller.*
11. Mazurka. Opus 6, No. 1............................*Chopin.*
12. Spring Song............................*Heller.*
13. Ecossaisen. Opus 33, No. 2............................*Schubert.*
14. La Brunette Valse............................*Egghard.*
15. Baby Bye. 4 hands............................*Mason.*
16. Don Juan (La ci darem). Arranged by Ketterer............................*Mozart.*
17. Gems from Schubert............................*Schubert.*
18. Les Deux Anges. Arranged by Berg............................*Blumenthal.*
19. Thunder and Lightning Polka............................*Strauss.*
20. Ecossaisen. Opus 67, No. 1............................*Schubert.*
21. La Fille de Madame D'Angot. Arranged by Cramer............................*Lecocq.*
22. Faust (Old Men's Chorus and March). Arranged by Sidney Smith............................*Gounod.*
23. Soldiers' March............................*Schumann.*
24. Fairy Polka............................*Spindler.*
25. Melody............................*Rubenstein.*
26. Jolly Brothers' Galop............................*Budik.*
27. Warblings at Eve. 4 hands............................*Richards.*
28. Wedding March............................*Mendelssohn.*
29. La Belle Helene. Arranged by Godfrey............................*Offenbach.*
30. Fra Diavolo. Arranged by Krug............................*Auber.*
31. Little Hunting Song............................*Schumann.*
32. Reminiscence of Mignon. Arranged by Berg............................*A. Thomas.*
33. Curious Story............................*Schumann.*
34. Girofle–Girofla Lanciers. Arranged by Claude............................*Lecocq.*
35. Sonato Facile............................*Beethoven.*

VOCAL.

36. Let Me Dream Again............................*Sullivan.*
37. You and I............................*Claribel.*
38. Esmeralda. Gipsy Song............................*Levey.*
39. Looking Back. Song............................*Sullivan.*
40. The Danube River. Ballad............................*Aide.*
41. Good Night, Farewell. Song............................*Kucken.*
42. Sweet Echo Dell............................*Work.*
43. Marjorie's Almanac. Ballad............................*Charlotte Sainton Dolby.*
44. The Mandolin. Serenade............................*Connolly.*
45. Little Bo-Peep. }
46. The King of France. } Nursery Songs.
47. Jack and Jill. }
48. Three Children Sliding. }
49. My Lady Wind }
50. The Storm. Descriptive Song............................*Hullah.*
51. Softly now the Light of Day. Quartette............................*Weber.*
52. The Jewish Maiden. Song............................*Kucken.*
53. Johnny Morgan. Song and Chorus............................*Read.*
54. The Ivy Green. Song............................*Russell.*
55. Nancy Lee. Song and Chorus............................*Adams.*
56. Clochette. Ballad............................*Molloy.*
57. The Brook. Song............................*Dolores.*
58. Rocked in the Cradle of the Deep. Song............................*Knight.*
59. Bethlehem. Shepherds' Nativity Hymn............................*Gounod.*
60. Terzetto. Lift Thine Eyes. From Elijah............................*Mendelssohn.*
61. O Rest in the Lord! Solo............................*Mendelssohn.*
Charades for Parlor Performance............................*H. L. Wait.*

FACTS ABOUT THE STRATTON VIOLINS.

The great success that has attended my selection and sale of STRATTON VIOLINS is easily explained.

1st. They are scientifically made, and therefore improve much more rapidly than any similar priced violins, made by hand, can possibly be expected to do.

2d. By the use of machinery in cutting out the tops and backs, Mr. Stratton not only produces a perfect model of the old Cremonas, but does it at a price that brings a fine-toned Violin within the reach of all.

3d. It is well known that violins made of the same materials, and in precisely the same way, nevertheless differ widely in tone. With thirty years' experience in the use and sale of violins, during which time I have imported many thousands, and personally selected, for friends and customers, many hundreds, and with the only very large stock of Stratton Violins to select from, which I do by actually tuning to concert pitch and testing by tone and every other way, it would be strange if I could not give the purchaser a better violin for his money than he is likely to get anywhere else.

4th. I send them by express to all parts of the country, on a plan that not only relieves the purchaser of all risk, but absolutely insures him a profit!

The Result is What Might be Expected.

Every instrument sold improves so rapidly that after a year's use the purchaser has never, in a single instance, come back to me for his ten per cent advance, simply because, in every case heard from, he then regards his violin worth two or three times its cost. As this is rapidly becoming known from Maine to California, and from Minnesota to Texas, this branch of my business increases at a very rapid rate.

MY PLAN.

From the large stock of John F. Stratton & Co., in this city, I personally select by *tone, materials, trimmings, and finish,* three grades of the Stradivarius model, as best suited to the wants of the American people, as follows:

No. 1.—Violin for the Million, with complete outfit —bow, wooden case, rosin, and extra set of Olarabella strings $5.00

No. 2.—Violin for Amateurs, with complete outfit— bow, wooden case, rosin, and extra set of Olarabella strings 10.00

No. 3.—Violin for Artists, with complete outfit— bow, wooden case, rosin, and extra set of Olarabella strings ....$16.00 to 25.00

So confident am I of the rapid improvement of these STRATTON VIOLINS, that if any one who purchases one of my selection, and uses it steadily at concert pitch for one year, is willing to sell it, I WILL THEN PAY HIM TEN PER CENT MORE THAN IT COST HIM; or, if the purchaser prefers his own judgment to mine, backed by the foregoing offer, I will send a violin to him by express, C. O. D., with instructions to the express agent to hold the money six days, and if in this time the purchaser brings back the violin dissatisfied, he is to return the money to the purchaser and the violin to me at my expense.

To those wishing to Purchase.

Don't stop, as many do, to ask if the above offer still holds good. CERTAINLY IT HOLDS GOOD; and any correspondence on that point is a waste of time and postage.

The $5 Violin is far superior in tone to any thing ever before offered for the money, but, of course, the higher you can afford to go the better you will be pleased.

As I leave every one to adjust for himself the position of the sound-post, height and shape of bridge, etc., don't make up your mind the first time you draw the bow upon it. Three or four days' use sometimes changes first impressions. For example: A few days ago, Isaac C. Brown, Poynett, Wis., ordered a No. 2 Violin. When it first came he thought it was not as good as he wanted, and he ordered a No. 3. Three days latter he countermanded this order because the No. 2 had improved so much in that time.

TESTIMONIALS.

I could add the strongest testimonials from different parts of nearly every State and Territory of the Union, where Stratton Violins of my selection are now in use; but I have space only for the following from prominent persons, who will be recognized as experts, and whose opinions about a violin are entitled to great weight:

From CHAS. T. WORK, a brother of Henry C. Work, author of "Grandfather's Clock," and other popular songs.

Mr. C. M. CADY: DEAR SIR: I have pleasure in stating that I purchased, nine months ago, one of your $10 "*Stratton Violins,*" and it has improved so rapidly that I would not accept $30 for it if I could not procure another. It is certainly the best instrument for the money I ever used.

Yours, **CHAS. T. WORK,**
Queen Insurance Co., 214 and 216 Broadway, New York.

From JAMES BAXTER, Founder and Director of the "Baxter University of Music," author of "The Praise," and various musical text-books developing his "New School of Music."

Mr. C. M. CADY: DEAR SIR: Having kept one of your No. 3 "*Stratton Violins,*" for my own use during the last eighteen months, I am free to say that I am no less pleased with its improvement than I was surprised with the quality of its tone for the price, when it was first received; and except for the confidence that you could readily replace it, I would not be willing to part with it for double its original cost.

JAMES BAXTER, Friendship, N. Y.

From JAMES ROSCOE, Leader of "Roscoe's Orchestra."

Mr. C. M. CADY: DEAR SIR: Last August I purchased a "*Stratton Violin,*" of your selection, with a box, bow, and set of strings, for $5. In my own town the box would have cost me $3.50, the bow $1, and the extra strings $1, amounting in all to $5.50; so, in fact I got the violin for nothing, and it has so improved that it could not be bought to-day for less than $15. I bought a "*Stratton Violin*" for $10 two years ago, and to-day it is valued at $40 by good judges. I also know of a "*Stratton Violin*" that was purchased by a young man in Sherman, Pa., for $15, which, after being used one month, was pronounced by Prof. Marsh Hammond, a fine soloist, to be worth $100. To the best of my knowledge, the "*Stratton Violin*" is the best and cheapest violin in the United States.

JAMES ROSCOE, Titusville, Crawford Co., Pa.

From JOSEPH CATO, Quadrille Band Leader.

Mr. CADY: DEAR SIR: I have never handled the equal of the "*Stratton Violin*" which you sent me last fall, and I have had occasion to use a great many violins. I have played from 8 o'clock in the evening until daybreak on this violin, without experiencing half the fatigue which I have suffered with other violins.

JOSEPH CATO, Wakefield, Lancaster Co., Pa.

From GEO. W. WALTER, Son of Wm. H. Walter, Mus. Doc., New York City.

U. S. TREASURY DEPARTMENT, WASHINGTON, D. C.

Mr. C. M. CADY: DEAR SIR: In the short space of three weeks, the two new $25 "*Stratton Violins*" have marvellously improved, with only ordinary use. Both instruments are totally different in tone color, yet each seems perfection of its kind. With one year's use, I believe that you yourself would hardly recognize the originals. $50 could not re-purchase either of them; therefore no wonder you can afford to take them back in a year and refund the price, with ten per cent. premium. With thanks for your taste evinced in their selection, I am,

Very truly yours,

GEO. W. WALTER.

From DABIE YOUNG, Orchestra and Band Leader.

Mr. C. M. CADY, New York: DEAR SIR: The $16 "*Stratton Violin*" which you selected and sent to me about ten months ago has improved wonderfully. I had it tested a few days after I received it, by practical violinists, who guessed its cost from $25 to $30, and were surprised on hearing how cheap it was. It has turned out to be a perfect jewel, and I estimate its value to-day at $50. Yours truly,

DABIE YOUNG, Somerset, Ky.

From M. L. AVERILL, Violin Teacher, etc.

Mr. C. M. CADY: SIR: The "*Stratton Violin*" you sent me last January is a tip-top instrument, and considering the amount it cost here ($17.50), it is a very cheap instrument. It is improving in tone very fast, and is considered nearly equal to an $80 violin here, and, in my opinion, has a more brilliant tone.

M. L. AVERILL, Ohio Station, Bureau Co., Ill.

Mr. C. M. CADY: DEAR SIR: The $5 "*Stratton Violin*" which I bought of you nine months ago has improved in tone very fast. I could not buy as good a violin in a Western music store for less than $15 or $20. Yours respectfully,

A. E. HEMICK, Trenton, Ill.

Mr. C. M. CADY: DEAR SIR: No doubt you will remember that I sent to you for a violin last November. You sent me one of your No. 2 "*Stratton Violins,*" with good case, bow, rosin, and strings, for $10. I will say that I am well pleased with it, and consider it worth $25 to-day. I can recommend these violins to any one who wants to get a good one.

W. A. STEVENS, Emmettsburg, Iowa.

Mr. C. M. CADY: DEAR SIR: I have the pleasure to state that the "*Stratton Violin*" I bought of you for $11, in June last year, is improving very fast in clearness and strength of tone, and that it would take a large advance upon its cost to induce me to part with it. Yours truly,

Dr. JOOST ROELOFSZ, Pella, Iowa.

Mr. C. M. CADY, 107 Duane Street, New York; DEAR SIR: The "*Stratton Violin*" which I bought of you in December last cost me about $19. It has rapidly improved in tone, and I am highly pleased with it. I have used it about three months, and it improves more rapidly than any violin I have ever had. Wishing you success, I remain,

Yours truly, **H. ROELOFSZ,** Pella, Iowa.

Mr. C. M. CADY: DEAR SIR: The "*Stratton Violin*" I purchased from you more than a year ago, that cost me only $5, has improved very rapidly since that time. To-day I would not take $25 for it, particularly if I could not get another like it. I am perfectly satisfied that the "*Stratton Violin*" is the best that is manufactured.

W. H. HARRIS, Henderson, N. C.

Mr. C. M. CADY: DEAR SIR: It affords me no small amount of pleasure to say that the $5 "*Stratton Violin*" bought of you last October is the best one at any thing like the price I ever saw. I have paid as high as $15 for a much poorer one in your city. It has improved more in use than any violin I have ever heard. Yours truly,

W. H. WELCH, Ellijay, Ga.

LATEST SHEET MUSIC.

Vocal.—THE FIRE-BELLS ARE RINGING. The latest new song and chorus by Henry C. Work, with splendid portrait of the author. With fire bell accompaniment, it is irresistible.

"One, two, three—hark, hark, boys!
  One, two, three, four!
The fire-bells are ringing, this wild wintry night;
  They ask aid for District Thirty-four.
There somebody's riches are now taking flight;
  On flame-wings away—away they soar.
But hark! with shriek and wail how raves the gale,
  Like demon steeds it speeds—like galloping gangs from Pandemonium hurled.
Yet, firemen, take courage! Did valiant deeds avail,
  Then you were the victors of the world!

CHO. Ring the bells again! Wake the electric wire!
  And flash abroad the warning words, "Fire! Fire!"
    God save the city, for man's devices fail
  When fierce flames with wintry winds conspire.
    But hark! with shriek and wail," etc.

To represent the fire-bell in a public performance, a hotel gong is best, if it be in tone, *i.e.,* if it be sung in A flat, the gong must be A flat, C, or E flat.

WE SHOULD LOVE EACH OTHER MORE. Song and Duet, or Song, Duet and Chorus. Words by E. R. Latta. Music by R. B. Mahaffey. Splendid and effective both in parlor and concert. Price 30 cents.

"We should love each other more, as we oft resolve to do,
When our dear ones, for a while, have been only out of view;
Or when on affliction's couch, moaning, suffering, they lay,
And we trembled for their fate, as we watched them night and day.
    CHO. We should love each other more,
      Than we ever loved before," etc.

NANCY LEE. Words by F. E. Weatherly. Music by Stephen Adam. An exceedingly popular sailor's song. E flat. Price 25 cents.

"Of all the wives as e'r you know, yeo ho!
There's none like Nancy Lee I trow, yeo ho!
See there she stands and waves her hands upon the quay;
An' every day when I'm away, she'll watch for me,
An' whisper low, when tempests blow, for Jack at sea.
  Yeo ho! lads, ho! Yeo ho!
    CHO. The sailor's wife the sailor's star shall be,
      Yeo ho! we go across the sea,
      The sailor's wife," etc.

Instrumental.—LA BRISE (the breeze): VALSE DE CONCERT. By L. M. Gottschalk. E flat, 6. Price $1.00. This was written by Gottschalk just before he left New York for the last time, and given as a *souvenir* to his friend Mr. Chas. F. Sanger. Never before published. No doubt about its authenticity. Like some of the best of this great composer's other pianoforte compositions, it is strikingly brilliant and captivating.

THEMES FROM WAGNER'S "FLYING DUTCHMAN," including the celebrated "Spinning Song." Arranged for Piano by Alberto Human. Various keys. 3. Price 40 cents.

SEA-VIEW SCHOTTISCHE. For cabinet-organ or piano. Exceedingly popular and taking in style. E flat, 2. H. J. Heald. Price 35 cents.

The Great Selling Singing Book—THE WELCOME HOUR. By S. Wesley Martin and Wm. W. Walter, Mus. Doc. Contains the best inspirations of the best living composers—the genius and enthusiasm of the West and the culture of the East. It rapidly gains popularity with use. 1. Its Singing-school Department is alone worth more than 75c. 2. Its Chants and Tunes are alone worth more than 75c. 3. Its Anthems are alone worth more than 75c. 4. Its Concert Music is alone worth more than 75c. 5. Its Glees and Part Songs are alone worth more than 75c.

$7.50 a dozen. Sample copy, 75 cents.

"An exceedingly good music book * * containing nothing of a low grade."—*N. Y. Independent.*

"Good."—*N. Y. Christian Union.*

TEXT-BOOKS FOR "THE NEW SCHOOL OF MUSIC." By James Baxter, Founder of "The Baxter University of Music." Just published: **Practical Piano Culture. Practical thorough Voice Culture.** Each, $1.25. Practical Voice Culture in Press. Music Teachers everywhere should examine this New System.

Issued April, 1878. **PRECIOUS JEWELS.** For Sunday Schools. By J. H. Leslie and R. B. Mahaffey. Combines *freshness and originality with simplicity.* Up with the times in **Words, Music, Quantity, Quality and Price.** A Marvel of Elegance and Cheapness. Sample copy mailed to any address, 20 cents; $1.80 per dozen; or $15.00 per hundred.

I have no time to answer questions of mere curiosity, but if you have the money and want to buy, write me, giving plainly your own name and post-office address, including County and State, and I will guarantee you perfect satisfaction.

C. M. CADY, 107 Duane St., New York.

THE FLYING DUTCHMAN.

(Der Fliegende Holländer.)

Arranged for the Piano, by ALBERTO HIMAN. Op: 60.　　　　　RICHARD WAGNER.

The Flying Dutchman.—3. HIMAN'S GRAND MARCH, as played by Gilmore's Orchestra. Price 40 cts.

The Flying Dutchman.—3.   SOPHIE'S BIRTHDAY WALTZ. Alberto Himan. Price 30 cts.

The Flying Dutchman.—4   EVERYBODY'S FAVORITE MAZURKA. Price 30 cts.

The Flying Dutchman.—8   THE MERRY MASKERS. (Two airs to be played at once by one performer.) Price 25 cts.

Recollections of a Music Box.

CAPRICE.

I had a little music box
My favorite tunes did play;
My cruel friends they teased me so,
I gave the box away.

Yet oft in mind the toy I see,
Though long past from my view,
And one sweet air it played for me,
I'll try and play for you.

WILLIE PAPE,
Pianist to the Royal Family of England.

Op. 27.

* The Soft Pedal to be kept down throughout the piece.

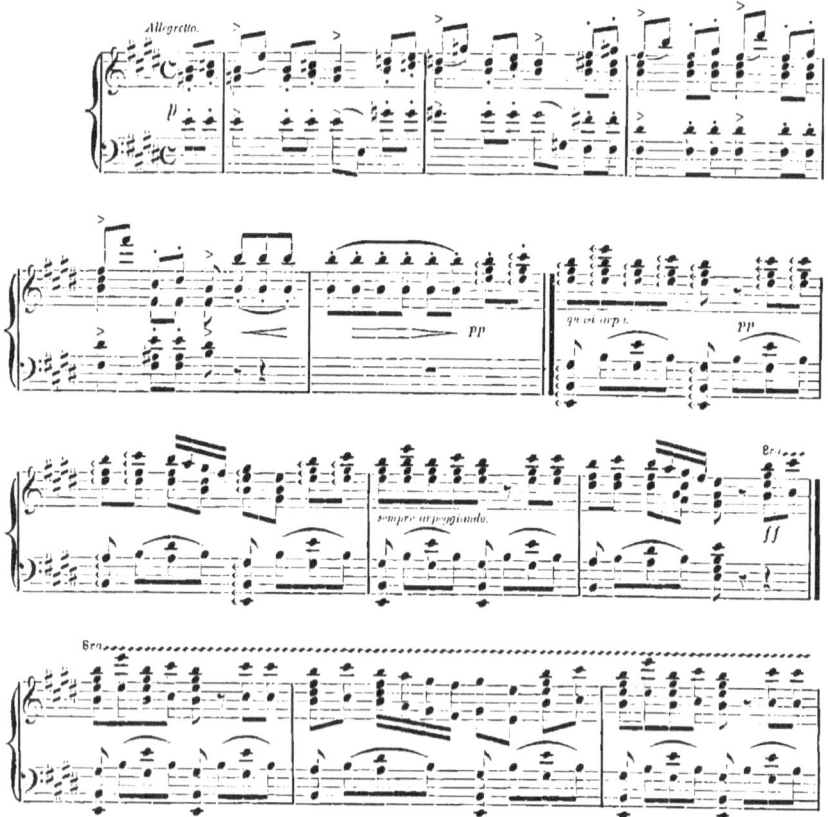

Amaryllis.-2.

ROMANZE.

ANVIL CHORUS.
IL TROVATORE.

Anvil Chorus.—3.

STRIDE LA VAMPA.

THE HAPPY FARMER.

R. SCHUMANN.

Op. 18. No. 2. ECOSSAISEN. SCHUBERT.

Beautiful Blue Danube Waltz.

(AN DER SCHÖNEN BLAUEN DONAU.)

Introduction.
Andantino.

JOHANN STRAUSS. Op. 314.

Danube Waltz.—5.

PETITE TARANTELLE.

Opus 46.
STEPHEN HELLER.

MAZURKA.

F Sharp Minor.

F. CHOPIN, Op. 6.

SPRING SONG.

STEPHEN HELLER.

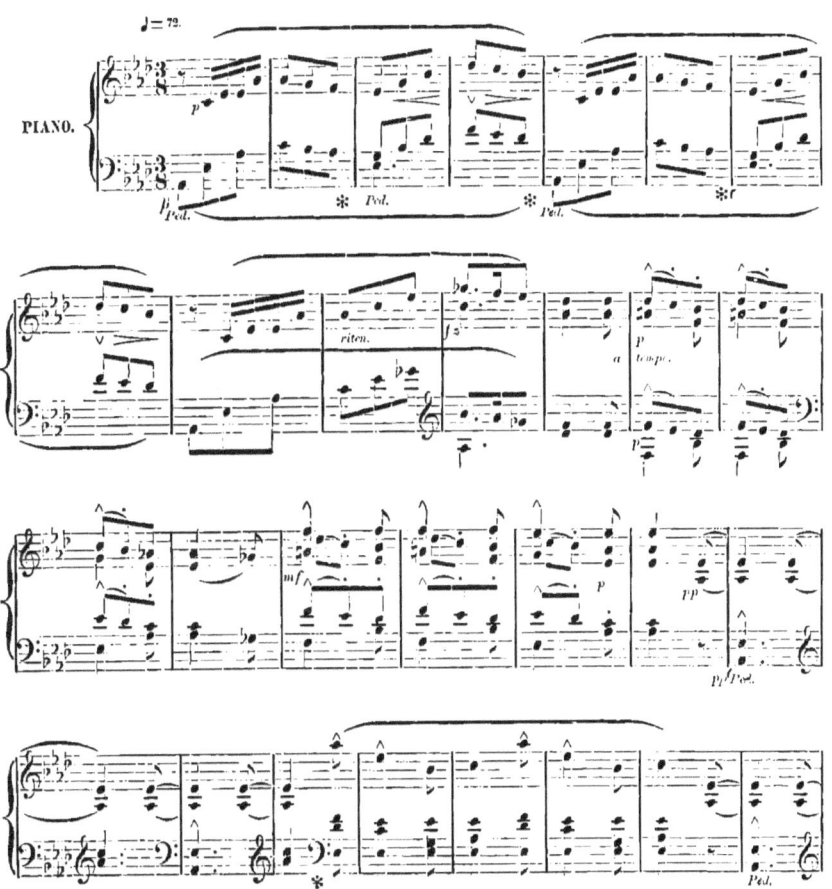

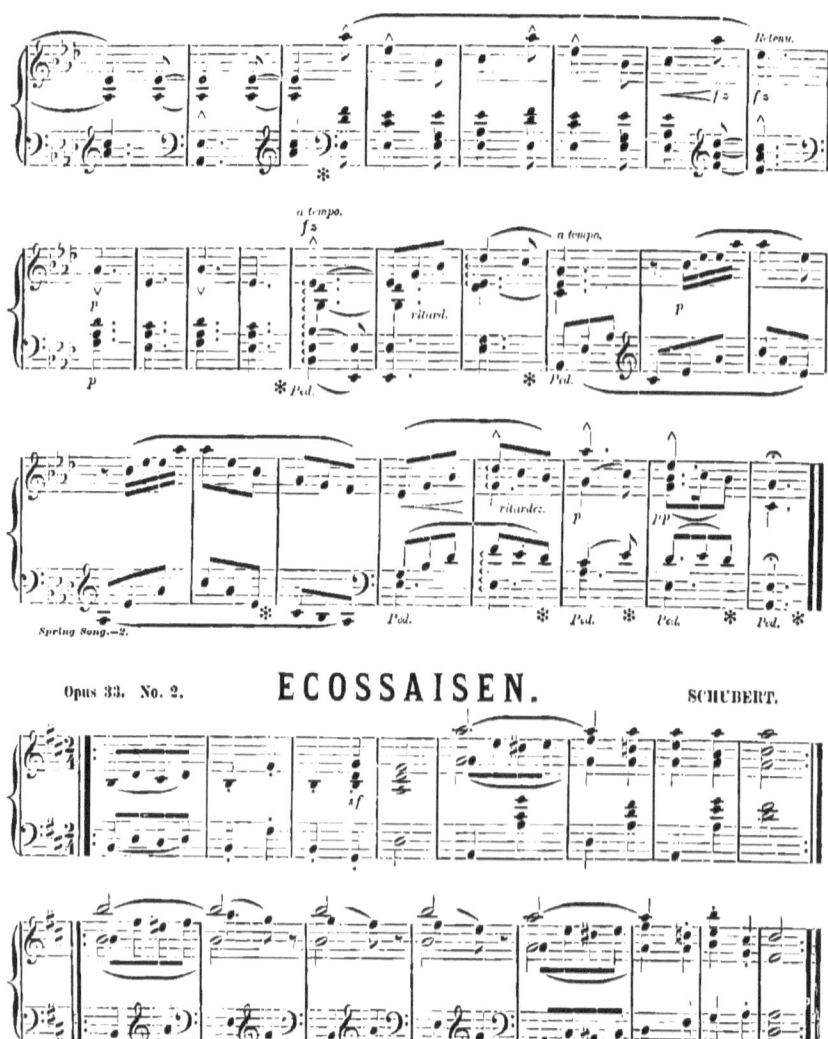

LA BRUNETTE.

WALTZ.

JULES EGGHARD.

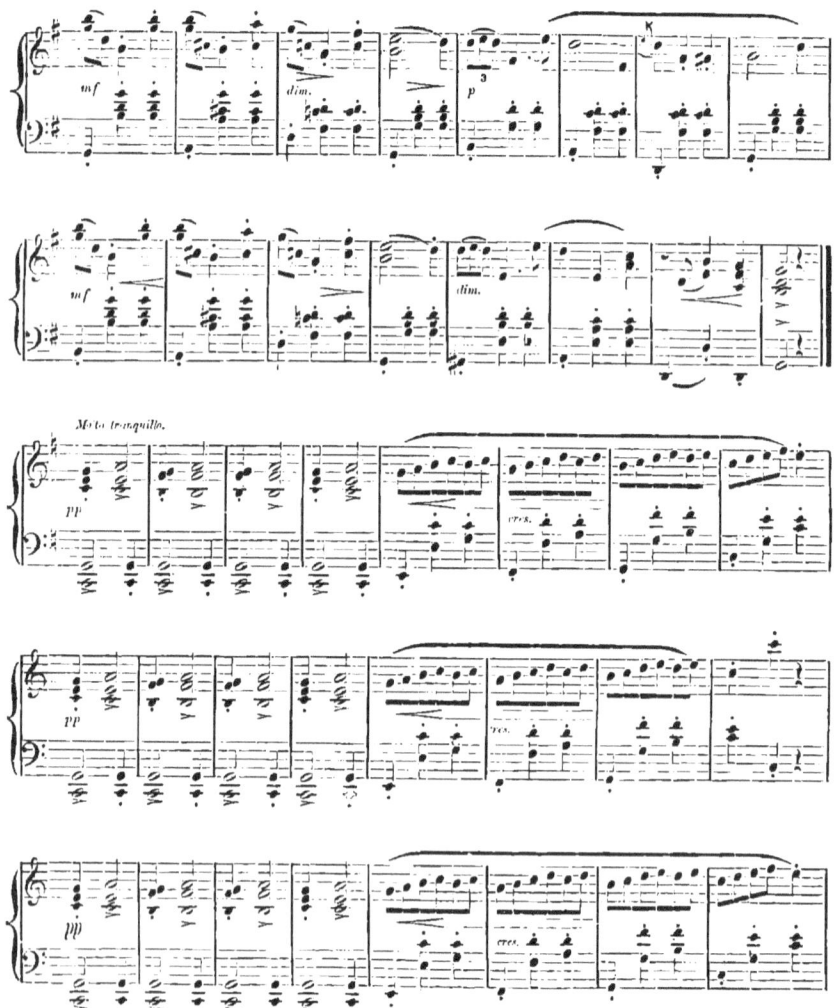

La Brunette Valse.—2.

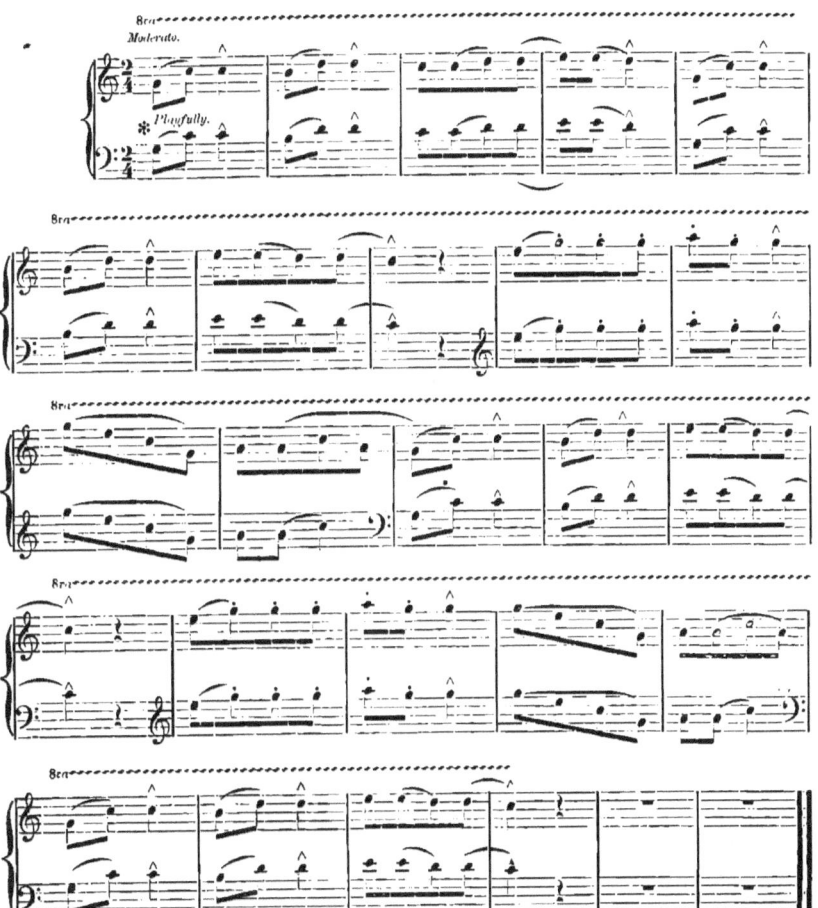

* The left hand of the "primo" player crosses over the right hand of the "secondo" player where the Bass clef occurs.

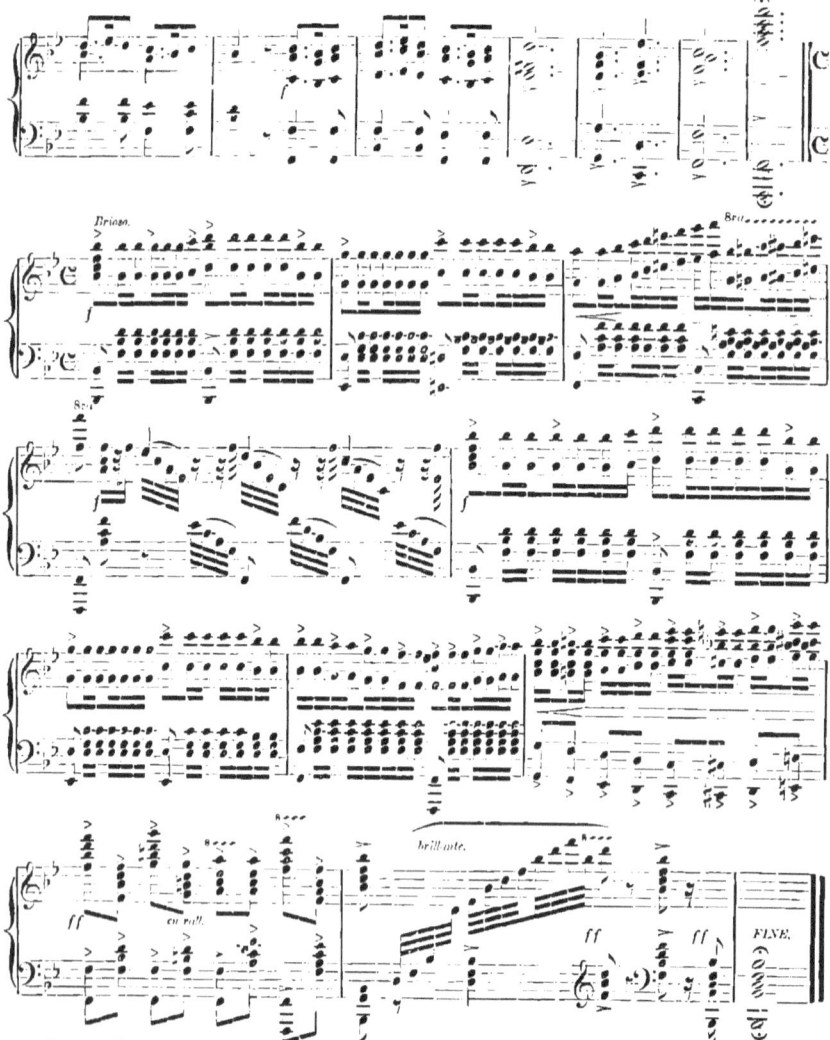

GEMS FROM SCHUBERT.

ECOSSAISEN. Opus 18. SCHUBERT.

LES DEUX ANGES.

(BLUMENTHAL.)

Varied by ALBERT W. BERG.

* By permission of S. Brainard's Sons.

FINALE.

THUNDER AND LIGHTNING.
(UNTER DONNER UND BLITZ.)
FAST POLKA.
JOHAN STRAUSS, Op. 324.

Thunder and Lightning.—3.

Thunder and Lightning.—4.

Thunder and Lightning.—5.

Opus 67. No. 1.   ECOSSAISEN.   SCHUBERT.

FAUST.

SIDNEY SMITH, Op. 117.

SOLDIER'S MARCH.

FAIRY POLKA.

Opus 93. F. SPINDLER.

MELODY.

ANTON RUBINSTEIN.

JOLLY BROTHERS GALOP.

(BRUDER LUSTIG.)

GALOP. F. BUDIK. Op. 10.

Jolly Brothers Galop.—2.

WARBLINGS AT EVE.
SECONDO.

BRINLEY RICHARDS.

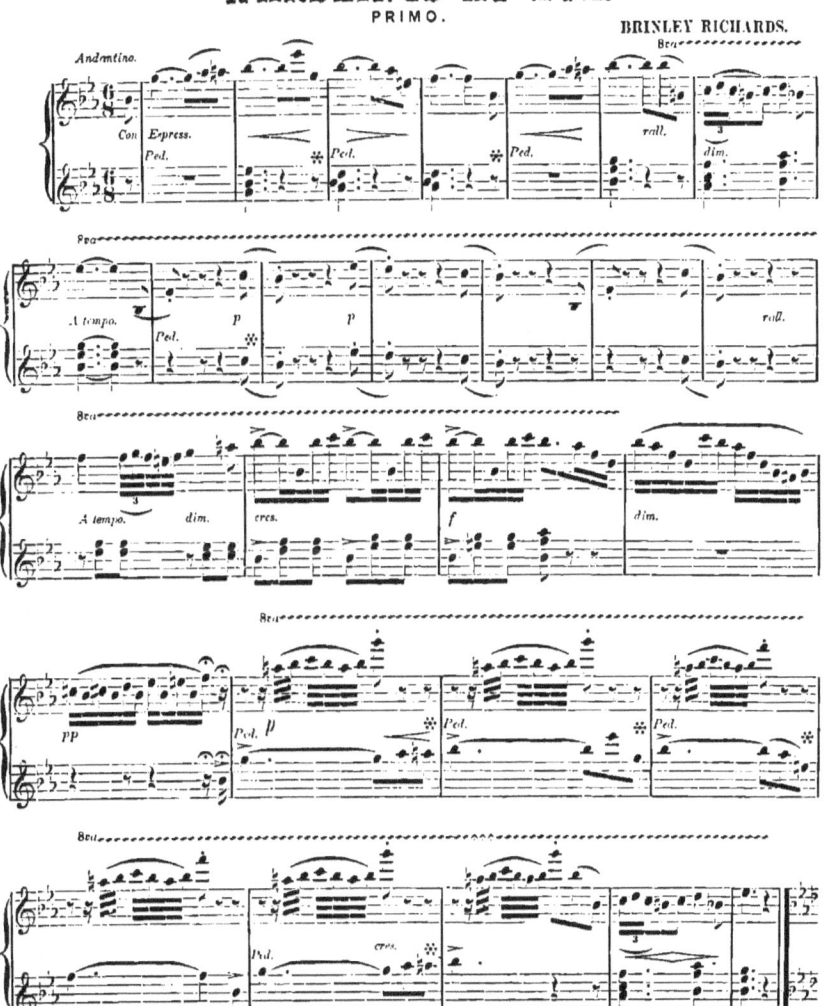

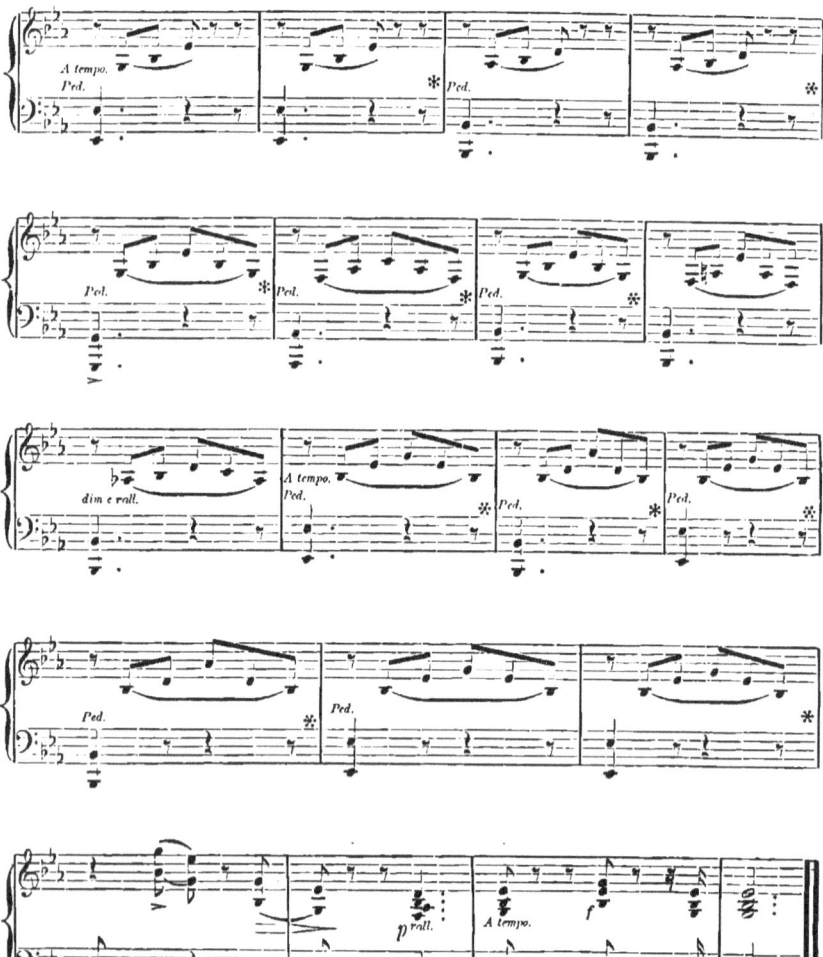

PRIMO.

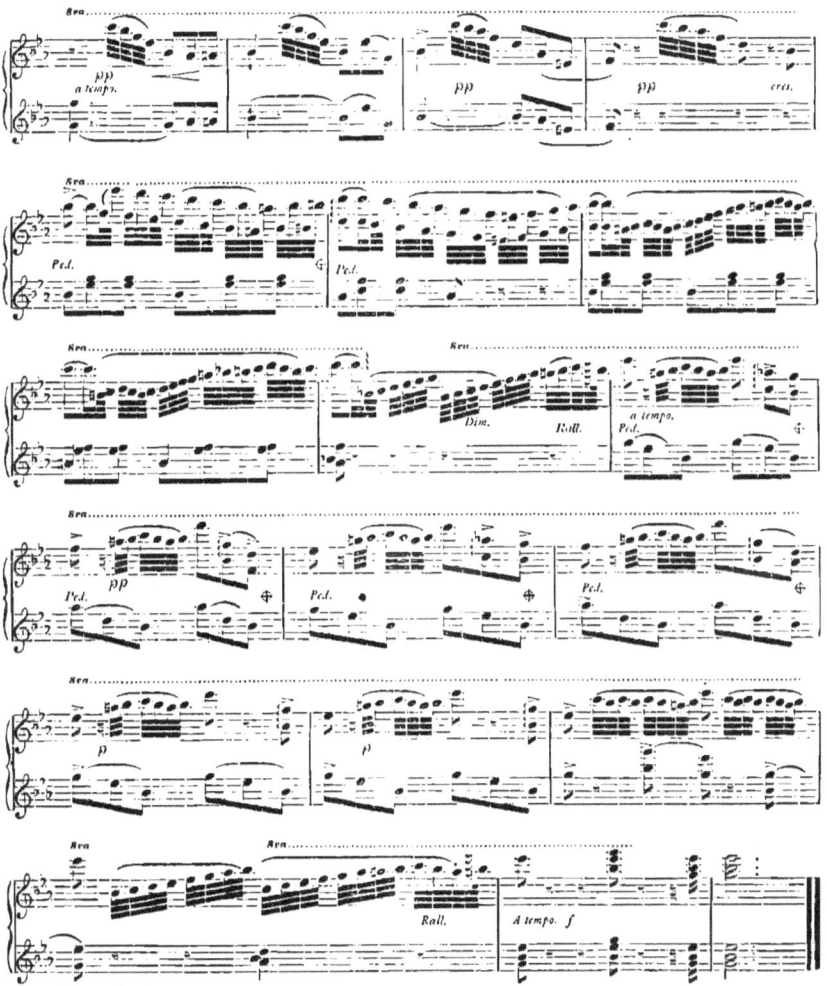

Warblings at Eve.—6.

WEDDING MARCH.

(MIDSUMMER NIGHT'S DREAM.)

MENDELSSOHN.

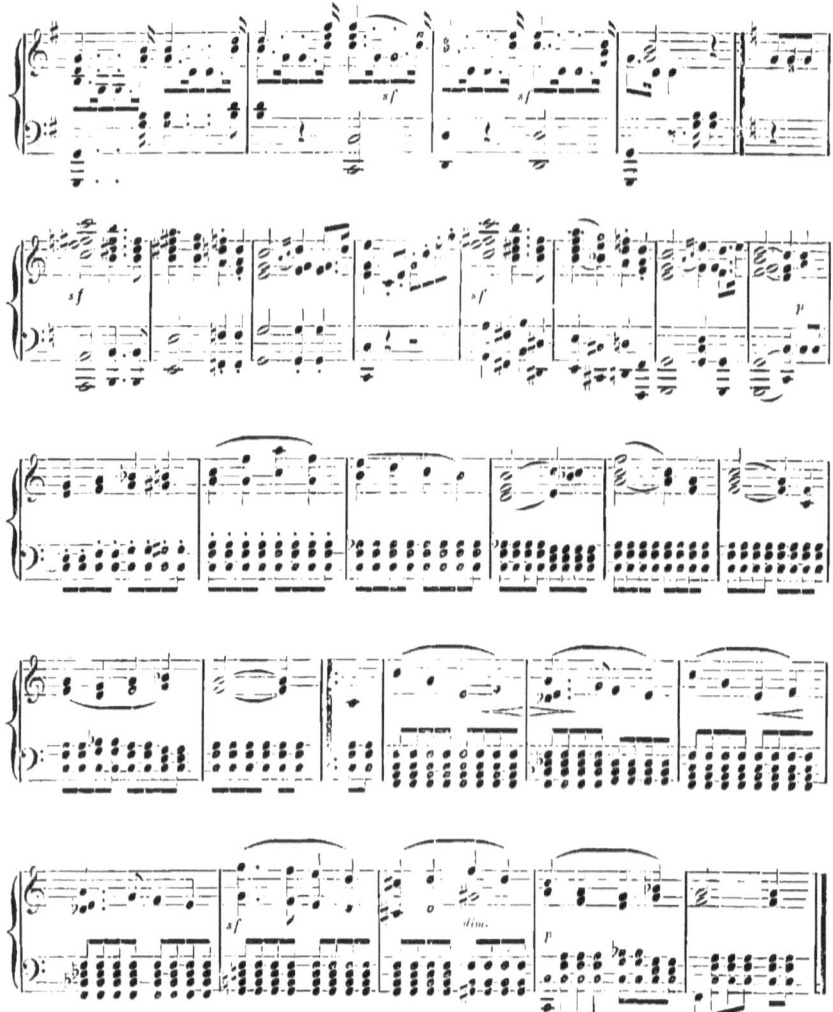

La Belle Hélène Galop.

Composed by OFFENBACH.   Arranged by D. GODFREY.

FRA DIAVOLO.

D. KRUG. Op. 123.

LITTLE HUNTING SONG.

(JÆGERLIEDCHEN.)

SCHUMANN.

MIGNON.*

A. W. BERG.

* By permission of Wm. A. Pond & Co.

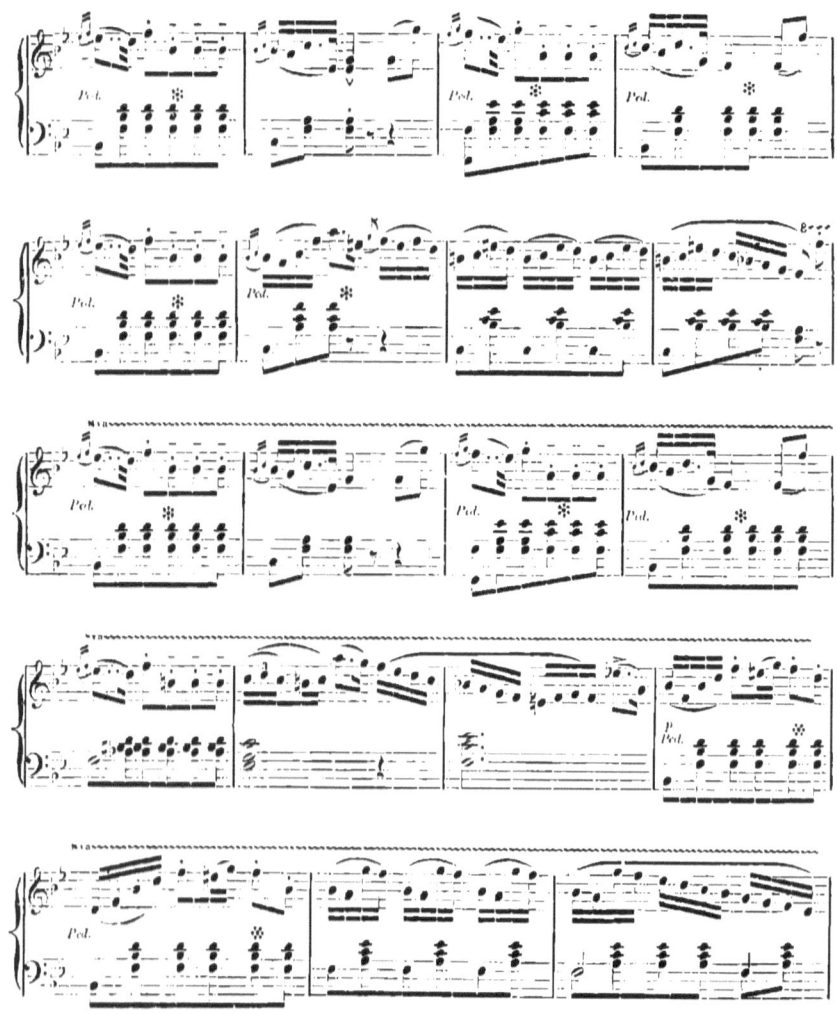

CURIOUS STORY.

SCHUMANN. Op. 15.

"GIROFLÉ-GIROFLA" LANCIERS.

(Opera by Lecoque.)

Arranged by CLAUDE.

* By permission of A. G. Slade & Co.

SONATA FACILE.

L. van BEETHOVEN.

LET ME DREAM AGAIN.

"YOU AND I."

Words and Music by CLARIDEL.

1. We sat by the riv-er, you and I! In the sweet sum-mer time long a-go.... So smooth-ly the wa-ter glid-ded by, Mak-ing mu-sic in its tran-quil flow; We threw two leaf-lets, you and I, To the riv-er as it wan-der'd on. And

2 'Tis years since we parted, you and I!
   In the sweet summer time long ago,
And I smile as I pass the river by,
   And I gaze into the shadowy depths below.
I look on the grass and bending reeds,
   And I listen to the soothing song,

And I envy the calm and happy life
   Of the river, as it sings and flows along;
For Oh! how its song brings back to me
   The shade of our youth's golden dream!
In the days ere we parted, you and I,
   As the two leaves were parted in the stream.

ESMERALDA.

Written by ANDREW HALLIDAY, Esq. Composed by W. C. LEVEY.

1. Where is the lit-tle Gipsy's home? Un-der the spreading greenwood tree, Where-ev - - er she may roam, Where-e'er that tree may be,...... Roaming the wide world o'er, Cross-ing the deep blue sea, She finds on ev'-ry shore, A home a-mong the free, She finds on ev'-ry

3. Oh leave her like the bird to sing, To sing.... on ev'-ry tree and bow'r, Oh leave her like the bee, To flit from flow'r to flow'r,... Roaming the wide world o'er, Cross-ing the deep blue sea, She finds on ev'-ry shore, A home a-mong the free, She finds on ev'-ry

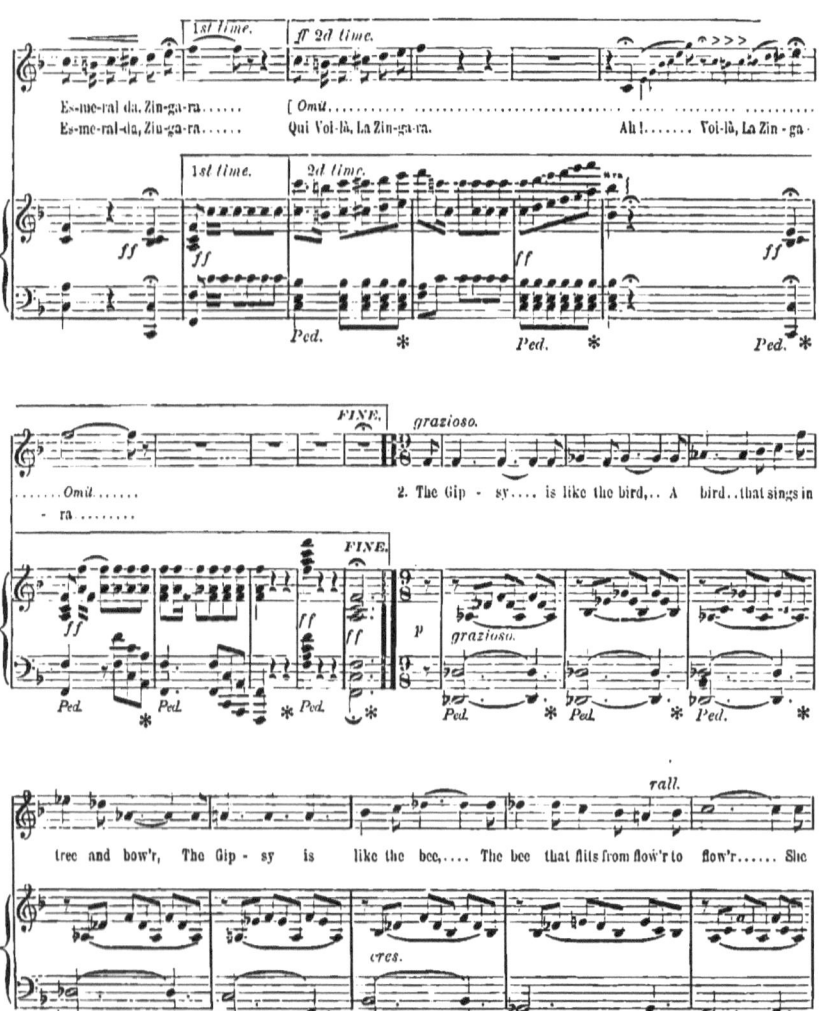

LOOKING BACK.

Words by LOUISA GRAY. Music by ARTHUR S. SULLIVAN.

To my Sister Etta.

SWEET ECHO DELL.

Three sons of a New England widow had long toiled in the Land of Gold, when this message reached them: "Come and see your mother before she dies!" They started immediately, but while crossing the Sierra Nevada the youngest became ill, and in a few hours breathed his last. He was buried in a lovely spot, near the summit. The mother lived long enough to greet her surviving sons; but her mind wandered, and she never fully realized that Willie had gone before.

Words and Music by HENRY C. WORK.

4 "Is he coming by-and-by?
  May I bless him ere I die?
Why then does he linger? Say, can you tell?"
  "Mirrored in that mountain lake,
  Heaven is near, and he will wake
Never elsewhere than in Sweet Echo Dell."—*Chorus.*

5 "Would you crush my only joy?
  Surely I shall meet my boy;
Why then does he linger? Say, can you tell?"
  "Never will his weary feet
  Travel more, yet may you meet
When your soul floats over Sweet Echo Dell."—*Chorus.*

Sweet Echo Dell.—3.

Little Bo-Peep.

NURSERY SONG.

The King of France.

NURSERY SONG.

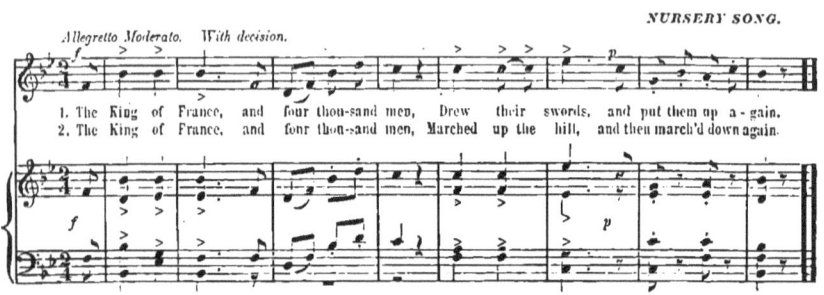

Jack and Jill.

NURSERY SONG.

Three Children Sliding.*

NURSERY SONG.

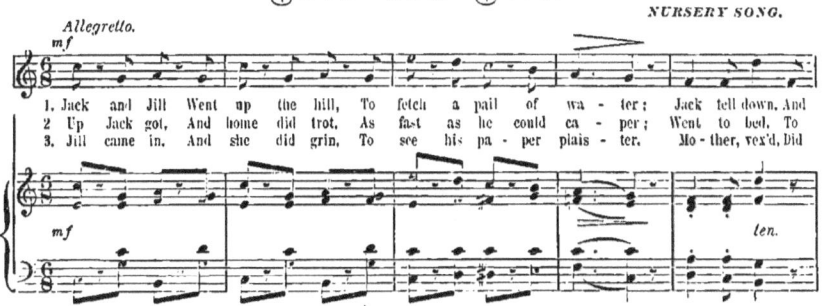

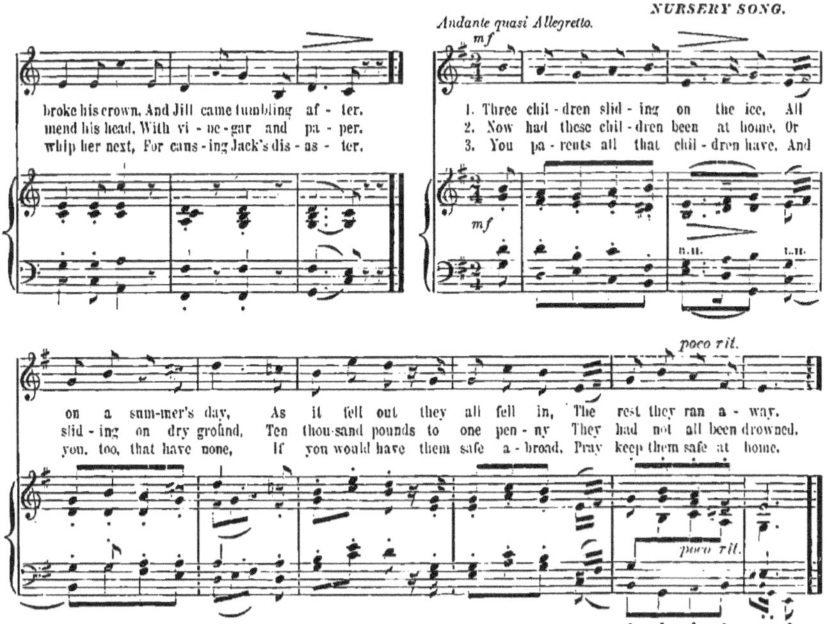

* May be sung as a Four-part Song.

"Softly now the Light of Day."

VON WEBER.

1. Soft - ly now the light of day Fades up - on my sight a - way;
2. Thou, whose all - per - vad - ing eye Naught es - capes, with - out, with - in,
3. Soon, for me, the light of day Shall for - ev - er pass a - way;

Free from care, from la - bor free, Lord, I would com - mune with Thee;
Par - don each in - fir - mi - ty, O - pen fault, and se - cret sin.
Then, from sin and sor - row free, Take me, Lord, to dwell with Thee;

THE IVY GREEN.

Words by "BOZ." Music by HENRY RUSSELL.

NANCY LEE.
SONG AND CHORUS.

Words by Frederick E. Weatherly, M. A. Music by Stephen Adams.

* As sung on board the U. S. Training Ship "Minnesota," with more than 300 boys and men.   * Pronounced KEY.

THE BROOK.

Words by TENNYSON. Music by DOLORES.

1. With ma-ny a curve my banks I fret, By ma-ny a field and fal low; And
2. I wind a - bout, and in and out, With here a blos - som sail-ing; And
3. I steal by lawn and gras - sy plots, I slide by ha - zel cov-ers; I

Rock'd in the Cradle of the Deep.

Words by Mrs. WILLARD. Music by J. P. KNIGHT.

BETHLEHEM.

THE SHEPHERDS' NATIVITY HYMN.

Written by HENRY FARNIE.   Composed by CHARLES GOUNOD.

TERZETTO.

To be Sung without Accompaniment.

"ELIJAH." By MENDELSSOHN.

O REST IN THE LORD.

ARIA.

"ELIJAH." By MENDELSSOHN.

THE WELCOME HOUR.

FOR USE IN

SINGING SCHOOLS,

CHOIRS, SOCIAL CIRCLES, MUSICAL CONVENTIONS, GLEE CLUBS, CONCERTS, Etc.

BY

S. WESLEY MARTIN and W. H. WALTER, Mus. Doc.

NEW YORK:
PUBLISHED BY C. M. CADY, 107 DUANE ST.

NEW SINGING BOOK.

The Welcome Hour.

By S. WESLEY MARTIN and WILLIAM H. WALTER, Mus. Doc.,

For Singing Schools, Choirs, Musical Conventions, etc.

$7.50 A DOZEN. SAMPLE COPY, 75 CENTS.

Both popular and classical, uniting the genius and enthusiasm of the West with the culture of the East. Fresh, original and beautiful, in words and music. Pronounced the best book for modern use published.

More than two years in course of preparation. Contains the best thoughts of the best living composers.

"An exceedingly good music book * * * containing nothing of a low grade."—N. Y. *Independent*. "Good."—N. Y. *Christian Union*.

Says a leading Convention conductor:—"I have now held two conventions with the 'Welcome Hour,' and I never found the work nearly so easy with any other book. The music seems to be so perfectly adapted for such work, while it is fresh and good. The 'Merry Blacksmiths' is one of the best concert pieces I ever used. It is immense with *awful* on the 'Pom, Pom' part." Says a classical music teacher of Philadelphia:—"I never saw so much good music in a book of the same size. All trash seems to be eliminated; and even the simplest Singing School music is inspired and beautiful!" The N. Y. *Christian Union* says:—"The music is simple, unpretentious and good. It meets that popular and growing taste, especially in the Church, for worshipful music." The N. Y. *Independent* says:—"It contains much of the Sullivan and Dykes order. We recommend it to schools, choirs and home singers."

1. Its Singing School department is alone worth more than 75c.
2. Its Chants and Tunes are alone worth more than 75c.
3. Its Anthems are alone worth more than 75c.
4. Its Concert Music is alone worth more than 75c.
5. Its Glees and Part Songs are alone worth more than 75c.

Send 75c. at once and get a sample copy.

BARGAINS IN STRATTON VIOLINS, CLARABELLA STRINGS AND CADY PIANOS.

C. M. CADY, 107 DUANE STREET, NEW YORK.

Charades for Parlor Performance.

KINDLY FURNISHED BY

HORATIO L. WAIT, Esq., OF CHICAGO.

ROMANTIC.—4 Acts.

CHARACTERS.—Mary and Annie, two merry girls. Tom and Dick, two jolly young fellows, and a comical old boatman.

RO

ACT 1.—A sofa or chairs covered with cloth being arranged like a boat and equipped with brooms for oars. The two girls are taken out to row by the two jolly fellows. They sing boat songs and enjoy themselves as if on the water, and then come ashore again.

MAN

ACT 2.—Mary and Annie in their bed chamber prepare to retire in a bed made of sofa, chairs, pillows, etc., sticking out from under which, conspicuous to the audience, is a pair of man's boots. The girls arrange their hair, put night-dresses on over their costumes, and just after getting into bed, while talking about the How and their beaux, discover that they have forgotten to blow out the candle. After much teasing Mary gets out to blow out candle, and before doing so, takes a look under the bed, and seeing the boots screams "a man," and both rush out screaming.

TIC.

ACT 3.—Old Boatman discovered growling because the jolly fellows have not paid him for the boat they hired of him, and copying Dick in the distance calls him. Dick enters and tries to persuade him to give him credit, or tick as the old boatman calls it, in which he succeeds.

ROMANTIC.

ACT 4.—Tom and Mary enter promenading in street dress. Stop to admire beautiful sunset, when Tom proposes to Mary and she accepts, when they go out. Then enter Dick and Annie promenading, who stop to admire sunset, when Dick pops the question and Annie accepts, then they go out. Then enter all four, who meeting, announce their mutual engagements, which on being explained, are pronounced as a very romantic coincident.

END.

DOMESTIC.—4 Acts.

CHARACTERS.—Mr. and Mrs. Prim, Miss Flora McFlimsey, Hon. Augustus Fitz Herbert Biddy O'Riley, and several servants.

DO

ACT 1.—Biddy O'Riley in a kitchen kneading dough, and groaning over the hardship of having to be maid of all work in a family of two, when young Mrs. Prim enters, and upbraids her with making away with the family provisions, and Biddy dares up, then Mrs. Prim scolds her for making bad bread, and Biddy wrathfully drives her out of the kitchen, packs up her old valise and band-box, and deserts the house.

MES

ACT 2.—Mrs. Prim discovered in her kitchen trying to make the dough Biddy left into bread, and is surprised by the entrance of the gorgeous Miss McFlimsey, who has walked through open doors unannounced. Miss McFlimsey is very airy and says she knows nothing about bread making, when Mrs. Prim says she has made a mess of her bread and asks for instructions, when the exquisite Augustus enters unannounced also, and escorts Miss Flora off for a drive.

TIC.

ACT 3.—Mr. Prim comes home in a hurry and finds his dinner not ready. Scolds and says he must always have it ready at exactly 5 to a tick. Mrs. Prim cries, and they have a scene, when he rushes off to advertise for a Domestic.

DOMESTIC.

ACT 4.—Mrs. Prim in her parlor, and the door-bell rings, when she admits a green Irish girl, who applies for a situation in answer to the advertisement. Then a Dutch girl comes, then an Irish girl, then a French girl comes, then an English girl, and so on. END.

MERCENARY.—4 Acts.

CHARACTERS.—Old Mr. Croesus, Mrs. Croesus, Miss Columbia Croesus, Captain Flyaway Dash (formerly Jonathan Nash), Old Prudence Nash, passengers on steamer, etc.

MER

ACT 1.—Old Mr. and Mrs. Croesus discovered studying over a guide-book in a Swiss Inn, planning a visit to the Mer de Glace. He makes funny blunders in pronouncing names of places, and Mrs. Croesus more ridiculous ones in trying to correct him. They call in Columbia and wish her to go with them, but she seems in an abstracted mood, and pleads indisposition. As soon as the parents have gone, Columbia makes a signal out of the window to Captain Flyaway Dash, and then soliloquizes over her imprudence in encouraging such a rakish character as he seems to be. Enter Captain Dash, who encourages her. Expatiates on his great wealth and property in America, and persuades her to agree to run away with him, and he is very particular to make her promise to bring all her diamonds and valuables with her.

CE—(Sea.)

ACT 2.—Scene on the deck of an Atlantic steamer in rough weather. Passengers sea-sick, etc. Columbia has married Captain Dash, and divides her time between being sea-sick and listening to the Captain's bright promises of the fine things that await her on her arrival in America.

NARY.

ACT 3.—Columbia in her room at hotel in Boston. Wondering where the Captain has gone to, and having looked everywhere for her diamonds, wonders where they can have gone to. Enter Mrs. Prudence Nash and old Yankee woman, who wants to know if she is

THE NEW SCHOOL OF MUSIC.

"The better music is known and understood,
The more it will be valued and esteemed."—Moore.

Every one engaged in a course of musical practice, realizes the necessity for some intelligible form of understanding, some definite and practical basis of thought upon which to exercise independent judgment as to the propriety and excellence of their own and others performances.

The New School of Music seeks to supply this need by giving to learners study the same form and common sense and practical understanding of the people; rendering it plain and simple of apprehension, rapid in its attainment, and correspondingly satisfactory in its results.

FIRST PRINCIPLES.

The New School of Music recognizes the music principle as an inherent element of the mind, which, originating in the intuitive impulses of emotional action only requires development to be made to render it practically available on the natural language of the heart.

Recognizing then at the very source and fountain of musical action, and developing its inspirational impulses in practical relations in the exercising, the mind becomes a living principle of intelligible expression, in every transfiguration of which it is enabled to develop the inherent consciousness at every advancing stage of development as the subject is unfolded.

For the vocal performance the Voice is formed to tones of sympathetic or passional expression, developing the full power, beauty and resonance of the vocal tone and rendering its inspirational qualities intellectually available for effective expression in every performance.

For instrumental performance the execution is formed to the sympathetic touch of inspirational action in the use of the instrument, developing the full power and resources of the instrument and rendering it intellectually available for effective musical rendition.

With this form of culture the performance becomes imbued with a delivery of perception, depth of understanding and intellectual expression unknown to the mere performing musician.

"Words should be subordinate to ideas;
It is do not place the pedestal on the head of the statue."—Larpent.

Execution should be subordinate to musical ideas;
We do not copying music for the sake of the performer.

This new school of music is the result of more than twenty years of professional study, and experience in the education of a large number of students of music for the higher positions, and is believed to be the only one in which music is treated in its relation to our emotional and aesthetic perceptions. It will be found to meet the requirements of interpreting not only the best masters, of which it gives the key, but rendering the popular forms of modern composition as well; and making the subject of modern composition as well; and intellectually expressive as it consists intrinsic educational value, aside from its application to musical practice, in every branch of popular education.

The aim is to present music as a subject of intellectual thought and understanding, rather than as a mere matter of executive dexterity or as a code of rules to be observed in the execution, as is therefore confidently offered to the attention of the best educated musicians, as well as the amateur, or the student desiring personal improvement.

PRACTICAL STUDIES.

The following subjects of study comprise the educational practice of the "New School of Music," including the vocal as well as the instrumental. Each study is complete in itself, is easy and readily understood, and may be taken separately, or any two or more may be taken together in the order of their succession, or may be all taken at the option of the student:

1. "Voice Culture," is a course of practice in the formation and use of the voice, the perception of the tone qualities and their application in vocal exercises, by which it becomes available to the performer for easy and reliable use, and which can never create physical disturbance or disease in singing or in speaking.

2. "Piano Culture," is a course of practice in the formation and use of the touch, the perception of the tone qualities of the instrument and their application in piano exercises, by which the best qualities of the instrument are made readily available to the performer and their excellence preserved to the longest possible period.

3. "Musical Perception," is a course of practice in the sound, thought, and idea of musical effect; and the formation and perception of its sound.

4. "Musical Rendition," is a course of practice in musical execution, clarevoy, and the elegance of vocal and instrumental performance.

5. "Instrumental Culture," is a course of practice in the musical sounds and their notation, including all that pertains to reading the notes at sight, and constitutes the orthography and notation and of music.

6. "Thorough Bass Culture," is a course of practice in making and distinguishing chords by sight and sound, and its application in practical performance, and constitutes the cypher system of music.

7. "Literacy," is a course of practice in the construction and classification of chord effects and in the order of their relation in musical formulations. This is the syntax of music.

8. "Composition," is a course of practice in the use of chord effects, their development into musical thought and idea, and their arrangement into the form of finished compositions; and is the grandest of musical sciences.

Four of the above departments, viz.:—"Voice Culture," "Thorough Bass Culture," and "Musical Rendition," "Thorough Bass Culture," by James Baxter, E. K. Author of "The Praise," and other musical books.

PIANO CULTURE, by James Baxter .... Price.
VOICE CULTURE, by James Baxter $1.25
THOROUGH BASS CULTURE, by James Baxter 1.25
                                                    1.25

"Rudimental Culture," really belongs in many cases, as being the first branch of the Grammar of Music; but, as many wish to see the other books separately, the Rudimental part is inserted in all the above books. The above books mailed to any address on receipt of marked price.

It yet remains for the same author to treat of the four remaining departments, "Literature," "Musical Training," "Sympathy," and "Composition."

A book of Church Music, by James Baxter, consists of 384 full-sized pages, embracing a full variety of fresh, new music for Choir, Singing-School, and Festival uses, including nearly 100 pages of Anthems. The new feature of this book is a department of Anthems, Concert Glees, &c., arranged with orchestral accompaniments, such as can be played in almost every village, and which are alone worth twice the price of the book. Price $10 dozen. Sample copy, $1.

THE PRAISE,

PUBLISHED BY

C. M. CADY,

107 DUANE STREET,

NEW YORK.

CHARADES FOR PARLOR PERFORMANCE.

the young "gal" who has married her son Jonathan. After much misunderstanding, the painful truth comes out that Captain Dash is an unprincipled scamp and adventurer, and to all poor distressed Columbia's questions as to his alleged possessions, such as "Has he not got a rich copper mine at Lake Superior?" etc., Old Prudence reiterates the answer "nary", a copper mine, etc., etc.

MERCENARY.

ACT 4.—Captain Dash discovered gambling with an old gambling friend, for Columbia's diamonds. Enter Columbia, who storms and upbraids the Captain. Calls him a mercenary deceiver, and finally faints away. END.

SPELLUNACY.—3 ACTS.

CHARACTERS.—Old Dr. Bookworm, Mrs. Bookworm, Bella and Dora, his daughters, Tom and Dick, two students, and Spelling Class.

SPEL

ACT 1.—Old Dr. Bookworm discovered in his study, absorbed in studying a huge book. Enter his daughters, Bella and Dora, who ask for his dictionary, to find the word sy-zy-gy, that Tom has been telling them of, to see what it means, and how it is spelled. Old Dr. Bookworm enters into a learned disquisition upon the word, and orthography generally. Tom and Dick call, and are shown into the library. Make love to Bella and Dora. After having poked some fun slyly at Old Dr. Bookworm, and get him to hunt the dictionary through, in vain, in a very absorbed way, for the word lack-ache, which they spell out lac-ks-che, and ask him the proper pronunciation of. Dye and by the girls discover the joke, and the Old Doctor drives them all out of his study.

LUNACY.

ACT 2.—Mrs. Dr. Bookworm discovered mending stockings, and complaining about her family cares. Calls in Bella and Dora to help her. They talk enthusiastically about the spelling schools they have attended with Tom and Dick. The mother scolds them for being so intimate with these young scamps of students, when Old Dr. Bookworm enters, and in a very excited state, tells of a spelling match he has attended, and proceeds to unfold a grand scheme he has formed for revolutionizing the educational systems of the world, by means of competitive spelling matches. His wife tries to check him; says he is crazy, etc., but he makes out to make arrangements for his first match, and his wife, after moralizing over him, pronounces it a clear case of lunacy.

SPELLUNACY.

ACT 3.—A spelling match, presided over by Old Dr. Bookworm. Conducted in a ridiculous way, with as many participants as can be conveniently used. END.

PLATONIC.—3 ACTS.

CHARACTERS.—Mr. and Mrs. Grundy, Lucy Grundy, Homer Wise, a student, Farmer Granger and Wife, Bill Granger.

PLA

ACT 1.—Mrs. Grundy and Lucy discovered talking about getting up some private theatricals. Mr. Grundy engaged in reading newspaper. Mr. Homer Wise calls. Enters into the discussion, which becomes animated. Various plays are talked of, and extracts read or recited in an extravagant way, and so boisterously as to disturb the reading of old Mr. Grundy, from whom they receive gruff interruptions. The play of Romeo and Juliet turns the conversation to the subject of love, and Mr. Homer Wise talks learnedly of platonic love. Mr. Grundy makes satirical comments thereon. The Grundys tell Mr. Homer Wise they are going to spend the summer up in Maine, with Farmer Granger, and invite him to visit there.

TONIC.

ACT 2.—Old Mr. Grundy discovered seated in Farmer Granger's house. Wonders where all the occupants have gone to, and why his family don't arrive. Enter Farmer Granger, who salutes Grundy, and then goes mysteriously to closet and brings out a black bottle, and gives Grundy a drink, saying he keeps it for a Tonic, and cautions him about letting his wife or Bill know anything about it. Then goes out to hunt up his "old woman." Enter Mrs. Granger. She is rejoiced to see Old Grundy, and then after salutations, etc., goes to place of concealment and brings out another black bottle, and gives Old Grundy a drink, saying she likes to take a little Tonic for her stomach's sake, and cautions him not to speak of it to the old man or Bill. She then goes out to get lunch for Grundy and his family ready before the latter arrive. Enter Bill Granger, who greets old Grundy cordially,

and after salutations, goes to place of concealment and brings out another black bottle, and gives Old Grundy a drink, saying he keeps a little Bitters, for his health, and enjoins him not to let the "old man or old the woman" know anything about it. The Grundy family are heard arriving, and the two go out.

PLATONIC.

ACT 3.—Bill Granger discovered trying to do the agreeable to Lacy, but he is very awkward and unsuccessful. Lucy's thoughts are evidently elsewhere, and she seems to be expecting somebody. Suddenly Mr. Homer Wise arrives. Bill sees that he is not wanted, and leaves. Mr. Homer Wise and Lucy commence making love vigorously. Proposes and is accepted. They embrace. When suddenly Old Grundy and Farmer Granger appear. Grundy pretends to scold, and wants to know if that is what Mr. Homer Wise calls Platonic love. Old Granger holds up his hands in horror, and exclaims "What will Mrs. Grundy say?" END.

WASHINGTON.—3 ACTS.

CHARACTERS.—Mrs. Shoddy, Mr. Shoddy, Miss Susie Shoddy, Hon. Frank Subsidy, Member of Congress from Buncombe, and Mehitabel, his wife, several Senators, etc.

WASHING

ACT 1.—Mrs. Mehitabel discovered in her kitchen with a large washing, and her maid of all work has just deserted her. She must do it herself, and at once, as there is no laundry near and she is about to go to Washington with her husband who has just been elected to Congress. So she gets a tub and goes to washing, when old Mr. Shoddy suddenly enters through open doors, having rung in vain, in search of Hon. Mr. Subsidy. After some plain Yankee talk from Mrs. Subsidy, and much grandiloquent discourse from old Shoddy, he retires.

TON.

ACT 2.—Parlor in Mr. Shoddy's house. Mrs Shoddy and Susie talk about their expected visit to Washington and Susie sings opera airs. Ridiculously talks about "the Ton" and high life generally. Old Shoddy enters and tells how he found Mrs. Subsidy actually washing her own clothes, whereat the Shoddys are horrified.

WASHINGTON.

ACT 3.—Mr. and Mrs. Subsidy receiving at their house in Washington. Several Senators present talking up a "stealing scheme." Enter the three Shoddys who are presented to hostess, and finding her a little airy, the ladies twit her about her doing her own washing, and trouble is imminent, but they are interrupted by arriving visitors, when old Shoddy attracts attention and shows his ignorance of matters generally, except in the especial line of bribing Congressmen, etc. END.

DILUTE.—3 ACTS.

CHARACTERS.—Miss Seraphina Scroggs, Susie, her nurse, Miss Blonde, Adolphus Stubbs, and Dr. Pilute.

DI

ACT 1.—Miss Seraphina and Miss Blonde discovered in the boudoir of former. They with great mystery discuss a wonderful new hair dye. Afterwards talk about Adolphus, the adorer of Seraphina, and of his musical talent, when Miss Blonde terminates her visit and withdraws. END OF SCENE.

LUTE.

ACT 2.—Adolphus appears under Seraphina's window on a cold rainy night, clad in an old cloak made from a "waterproof," holding up a dilapidated old umbrella, and carrying a frying pan for a Lute to serenade his adored one. His ardor has been much dampened by the rain, and he has caught a bad cold and moralizes over his folly, but makes an effort to sing romantic songs and calls to his Seraphina. Suddenly old Scroggs' dog is heard barking, so Adolphus runs off.

DILUTE.

ACT 3.—Miss Seraphina discovered sick on a sofa, attended by Susie the nurse, who is being scolded in a petulant way because Seraphina caught cold while listening to serenade, and because the Dr. does not come. Finally Dr. Pilute, a comical old Homæopath, enters, and has quite a discussion with Seraphina about high dilutions, and prescribes a ridiculous dilution for her, which causes Susie to express her mind in a very indignant way and drive the Doctor out of doors, whereat Seraphina faints away. END.

www.ingramcontent.com/pod-product-compliance
Lightning Source LLC
Chambersburg PA
CBHW022114160426
43197CB00009B/1016